Abraham Lincoln

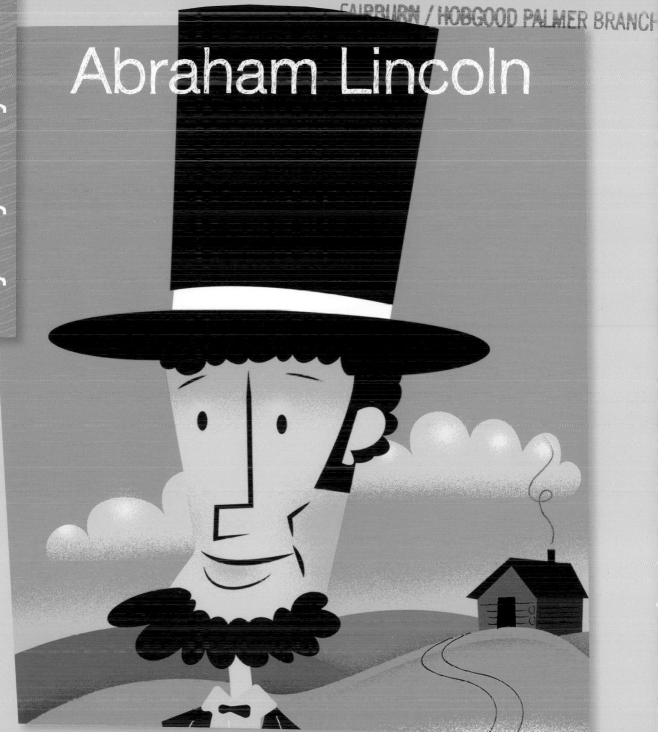

Published in the United States of America by Cherry Lake Publishing
Ann Arbor, Michigan
www.cherrylakepublishing.com

Content Adviser: Ryan Emery Hughes, Doctoral Student, School of Education, University of Michigan
Reading Adviser: Marla Conn, ReadAbility, Inc.
Book Design: Jennifer Wahi
Illustrator: Jeff Bane

Photo Credits: © Tom/Flickr, 5; © Internet Archive Book Images/Flickr, 7, 9; © Everett Historical/Shutterstock Images, 11, 20, 22; © H is for Hoosier: An Indiana Alphabet, illus. by Bruce Langton (Sleeping Bear Press), 13, 23; © Library of Congress, 15, 19; © B is for Battle Cry: A Civil War Alphabet, illus. by David Geister (Sleeping Bear Press), 17; Cover, 8, 14, 18, Jeff Bane; Various frames throughout, Shutterstock Images

Library of Congress Cataloging-in-Publication Data

Haldy, Emma E., author.
  Abraham Lincoln / by Emma E. Haldy ; illustrated by Jeff Bane.
    pages cm. -- (My itty-bitty bio)
  Includes bibliographical references and index.
  ISBN 978-1-63470-476-2 (hardcover) -- ISBN 978-1-63470-536-3 (pdf) -- ISBN 978-1-63470-596-7 (pbk.) -- ISBN 978-1-63470-656-8 (ebook)
  1. Lincoln, Abraham, 1809-1865--Juvenile literature. 2. Presidents--United States--Biography--Juvenile literature.
3. United States--Politics and government--1861-1865--Juvenile literature. I. Bane, Jeff, 1957- illustrator. II. Title.
  E457.905.H26 2016
  973.7092--dc23
  [B]
                                    2015026076

Printed in the United States of America
Corporate Graphics

table of contents

About the author: Emma E. Haldy is a former librarian and a proud Michigander. She lives with her husband, Joe, and an ever-growing collection of books.

About the illustrator: Jeff Bane and his two business partners own a studio along the American River in Folsom, California, home of the 1849 Gold Rush. When Jeff's not sketching or illustrating for clients, he's either swimming or kayaking in the river to relax.

I was born in a cabin in 1809.

I didn't go to school.
But I was smart. I liked to read.

I taught myself the law.

What would you like to teach yourself?

I liked books. I liked the Bible
and plays by Shakespeare best.

I fell in love with Mary Todd.

I married her. We had four sons. Only one lived to be an adult.

I became a **politician**.

I was elected president.

Would you ever want to be president? Why or why not?

America was divided over **slavery**.

The South fought **the North**. It was the Civil War.

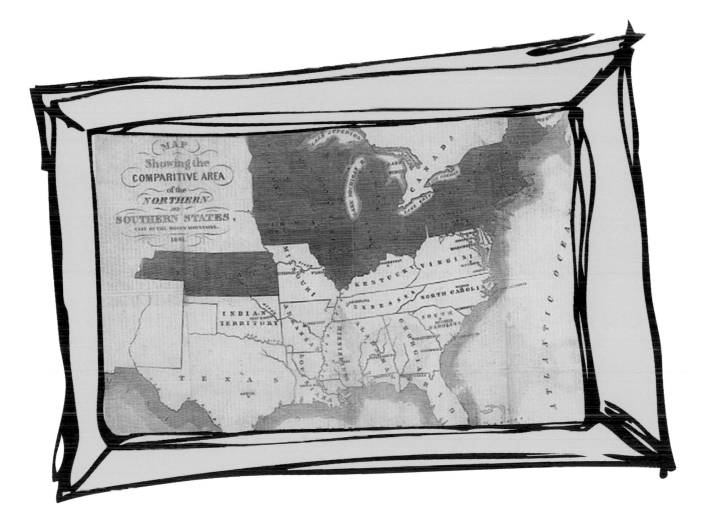

15

I wanted the war to be meaningful.

I worked to keep America united.

I worked to free slaves.

I wanted all men to be equal.

As the war was ending,
John Wilkes Booth killed me.

I was a great president.

I kept America united. I helped free the slaves.

What would you like to ask me?

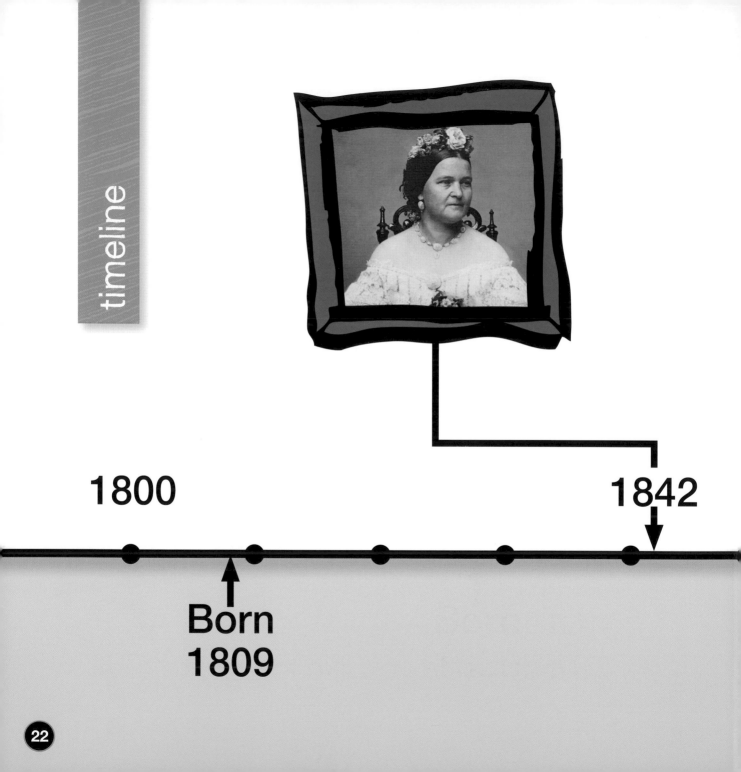

1800

1842

Born
1809

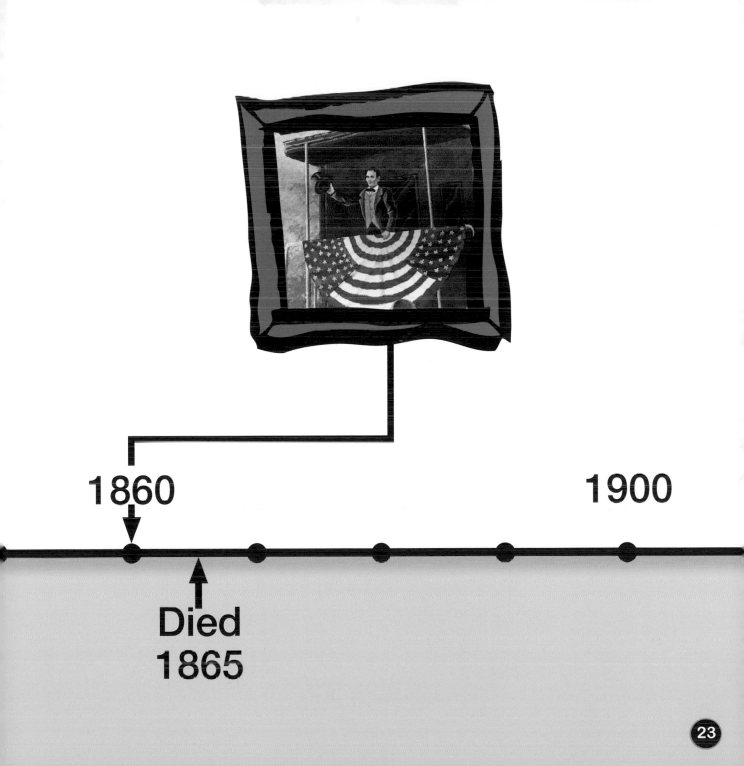

1860

1900

Died
1865

23

glossary

politician (pah-li-TISH-uhn) a person elected to the government

slavery (SLAY-vur-ee) the system of owning other people

the North (THUH NORTH) the states in the northeastern U.S. that did not have slaves

the South (THUH SOUTH) the states in the southeastern U.S. that supported slavery

index